C000047528

The Building of

HADRIAN'S WALL

by

ROBIN BIRLEY

ISBN 1 873136 07 2

© Robin Birley 1991

Published by: Roman Army Museum Publications,
Carvoran,
Greenhead,
Northumberland,
Via Carlisle
CA6 7JB.

Produced by A.R.P.
Newcastle upon Tyne (091) 234 2926

Frontispiece: Walltown Crags

Contents

Introduction

The remains of Rome's great north-western frontier across the narrow isthmus between the Solway Firth and the mouth of the Tyne have recently been designated a World Heritage Site. It is a proper tribute to what has rightly been described as the finest ancient monument this side of the Alps.

Hadrian's Wall is still something of an enigma. Its remains have excited the curiosity of scholars and antiquarians for the past three hundred years, but only a tiny fraction of the whole has been excavated and analysed. There are still many unanswered questions about the reasons for its construction, the purpose of the design, the nature of the garrison and the effect of the new frontier upon the province. Archaeological research will continue indefinitely, and every year another piece of the jigsaw will slot into place.

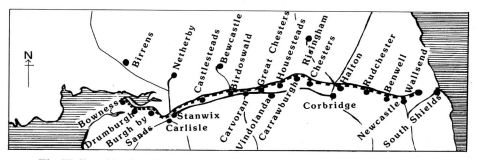

The Wall and its forts between the Solway Firth and the mouth of the Tyne.

Hadrian

Publius Aelius Hadrianus succeeded his kinsman Trajan as emperor in August A.D.117. He was a remarkable man. A stocky figure, a little above average height, with a fair skin and penetrating bluish-grey eyes, he was particularly conspicuous for his well-trimmed beard, setting a fashion which many thankfully followed. His father had died when he was only 10 years old, and Trajan assumed his legal guardianship. A few years in Rome brought him into contact with Greek learning, and he became a devout Hellenist, but his visit to his ancestral Italica in Spain allowed him to indulge in a passion for hunting and military exercises. Trajan summoned him to Rome again in A.D.93, treating him as a son. His education for public life followed, and he was to serve as tribune in three different legions - a record - and to experience at first hand

1

the complexities of Imperial administration. He accompanied Trajan on the great Parthian campaign of A.D.113, and whatever he thought about the desirability of an extension of empire in the east, the contact with a different civilisation stimulated his intellectual curiosity. Although he was never officially named as Trajan's heir, few doubted that he would succeed his kinsman, and he took over the empire in August 117 with comparatively little trouble.

It was a difficult time. The wars of Trajan had annexed fresh territories to an Empire which was already dangerously over-extended, and the Treasury was empty. Rome needed a man of far-sighted statesmanship and great organising genius to give stability and a breathing space: Hadrian supplied all that was wanted.

"Nature endowed him with manifold gifts, and he forced his talents to the upper limit" (Sir Ronald Syme), and his impact upon the Empire was to be lasting. He disliked pose and affectation, yet he had great pride and vanity, with a taste for magnificent architecture and the fine arts. He considered himself an expert in many branches of human endeavour, and he was never reluctant to give others the benefit of his advice. He was especially at home with his soldiers, and he was always happier in the camps of the frontier than in the lush palaces of Rome. A disciplinarian, he insisted that his armies should be highly trained and ready for any emergency, but he lavished praise upon those who he felt deserved it.

In a lifetime of travels, he spent only a brief period in his western provinces (A.D. 121-123), touring the defences of the frontiers. In Germany the army had seen no serious fighting for 20 years, and there were ominous signs of slackness. Hadrian's directives were firm. Luxuries were to be abolished, and there was to be no leave granted unless for urgent reasons. Any promotions were to depend upon military efficiency, good reputation and fairness in dealing with men. Officers' quarters were to be plainly furnished, and the men were debarred from tending fancy allotments near their barracks. "In a word, he so disciplined and organised the troops throughout the whole empire that his regulations remained the code for the army to this day" (Dio).

Hadrian's Visit to Britain

Hadrian's brief visit to Britain occurred in A.D. 122. The military situation there was difficult. A revolt had imperilled Rome's hold over the north, and casualties had been heavy. "The Britons could no longer be held under Roman control", claimed Hadrian's biographer. Commemorative coins issued in A.D. 119 recorded the successful conclusion of hostilities, and Hadrian may then have begun to plan a new system of frontier control. Some basic revision was essential. The Flavian and Trajanic system, based on the lateral Stanegate road and its support forts after the withdrawal from Scotland, was inefficient. There could be no question of another attempt at the complete conquest of the island, and the real trouble, in any case, may have lain in the Brigantian hills, already in theory subject to Rome. Throughout the Empire, the old days of expansion were over. Hadrian had already given up Trajan's eastern conquests and he examined the position of Dacia critically. He was now to assess the British situation. The province already had the largest Roman army in relation to its size, and the events of recent years had demonstrated that it would be unwise to reduce that strength.

The decision to retain Britain, in spite of its costly garrison, and to construct the most expensive frontier system in the Empire, may perhaps have been founded upon economic grounds, although prestige would have weighted heavily. Exports from the south of the province, such as corn and minerals, together with lead, silver and iron from the midlands and the north, and the wool and woollen garments from the southern farmlands, must have gone some way towards paying for both garrison and administration.

In the circumstances, Britain was probably worth more to Rome than many of her soldiers realised, and there was always the reasonable expectation that in due course the size of the army could be reduced.

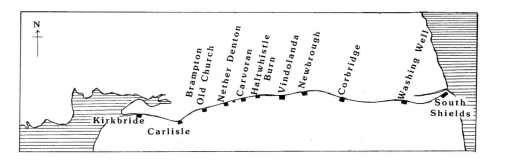

Trajan's Stanegate Frontier, with a series of forts along the road.

The plan to augment the network of auxiliary forts throughout the north with an artificial barrier from coast to coast was a bold one. The old soldiers in the army, who had themselves garrisoned Scotland before the withdrawal circa A.D.100, perhaps regarded this decision as a defeatist move. Veterans of Agricola's victory at Mons Graupius in A.D.84 - a few such men could still be serving - would remember the long campaign which took them to the shores of the Moray Firth, and must have commented upon the timidity of current Imperial policy. The army as a whole, which faced the task of building the new fortification, cannot have relished the prospect. All must have wondered where the Emperor had found the idea for such a frontier, but it was not unique. Although we have no positive evidence, it seems most likely that Hadrian had studied reports emanating from Roman merchants of China's great western wall.

3

Possible Influence of China's Great Wall

China's western wall had been built circa 100 B.C., and it was garrisoned until the end of the second century A.D., carrying out the dual role of defence, initially against the roving Huns, and of customs control. It was built of brick 320 miles long, and it had turrets at strategic points for signalling and observation purposes. Its garrison was made up in part of indigenous troops under their own officers, and in part by criminals settled in military colonies. As we shall see, its function and structure bear striking resemblance to Hadrian's Wall, and it seems a strange coincidence that two such barriers were erected at opposite ends of the earth. Although the first official contact between the Chinese and the Roman empires did not take place until A.D.166, Chinese records speak of western visitors to the court before that, and Macedonian merchants are known to be the source of information about the silk caravans from Serike, which passed through the Chinese Wall, which the geographer Ptolemy incorporated in his maps in the mid-second century. In addition the Han Annals record Chinese visitors to Parthia and Roman Syria in A.D.97. Any information about a military power beyond the feared Parthians must have been of considerable interest to Roman army commanders in the east, and reports based on such merchants' stories would have been sent to Rome and filed away for future reference. Hadrian may have come across the information when he was in the east with Trajan, and the narrow British isthmus may have given him the chance to attempt a similar scheme himself. He had the men and the necessary engineering skills at his disposal, and the geology of the area appeared to be suitable. A solution to the interminable British frontier problem might thus be found.

Planning and the Start of Construction

Hadrian's biographer leads us to believe that the Emperor planned the works himself when he visited Britain, probably in the summer of A.D.122, but it has been pointed out that our knowledge of the construction work suggests that an earlier start may have been made. It seems more logical to assume that the biographer erred in this matter of detail, and that army surveyors received their instructions in late A.D.119 or early 120. Their brief would be to find a site for a wall from coast to coast: their arrival on the Stanegate would have created furious speculation amongst the auxiliary forces already stationed there. The general details of the areas between Tynemouth and the Solway Firth were already well known, but the surveyors would have to test the nature of the subsoil, check upon the availability of suitable building stone, turf, lime and water, draw attention to the tactical view of alternative routes, and report on the nature of existing roads. One of their first observations must have concerned the availability of building materials. From the river Irthing to the North Tyne a wall of turf was out of the question, for the soil cover on the whin sill was too slight to provide the necessary depth of sod, but there was instead every facility necessary for stone construction - sandstone, limestone for mortar, coal in abundance for making the lime, sand, and timber for scaffolding. Further east lime would be more difficult to procure although the proximity of the Tyne would ease transport problems. West of the Irthing limestone was again a major problem, but it could be overcome if necessary, although in this region there was no shortage of excellent turf.

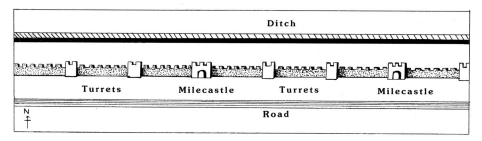

A section of the new frontier, as first planned. The forts were to remain on the Stanegate to the south.

Once the surveyors had sent their reports back to garrison headquarters at York, the staff would have to study the documents and turn them into a series of statistics and practical propositions. The comparative costs of alternative routes, the time factor, the number of specialists required if building was to be in stone, the transport problems and so on would have to be laid out clearly. Any form of Wall construction would create immense logistics problems: where were the builders to be housed, how were they to be supplied, and who was to protect them while work was in progress?

The crux of the matter must have been the political situation. Was the north sufficiently quiet to risk committing the greater part of the army to a massive building programme? And would that building itself generate an ugly military problem? York, with all its knowledge of years of frontier administration, could only advise: the decision lay with the Emperor.

It would seem that Hadrian made his decision by the middle of A.D.120, and work may have commenced either in that year or more likely in 121: at any rate, several months of advance preparation would be necessary before any form of construction could start. Quarries had to be located and opened up, and so had coal mines and sand-pits. Temporary roads had to be laid - a major and essential task - and the builders' quarters had to be prepared. It must have been a relief to the legions to know that there was no thought of their permanent removal to the Tyne-Solway gap: the garrison was to be formed around those already stationed on the lateral Stanegate road just south of the proposed line of the Wall.

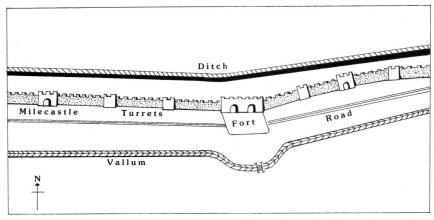

The revised plan, with forts on the Wall and the Vallum barrier to the south.

The Components of the Wall

At this point it must be emphasised that the series of fortifications now known as Hadrian's Wall were not all of one build, although ultimately they were all incorporated in the frontier. Excavation has shown quite conclusively that the original plan was modified more than once before the whole series was complete, and it would be as well to enumerate the various components before examining their constructional sequence, and the motives that lay behind the changes.

There already existed a network of roads, built by Roman army engineers, throughout southern Scotland - the relics of the 20 years of occupation from Agricola's campaign to c A.D.100. Of particular importance to frontier strategy were the two trunk roads, one stretching north from Carlisle to the Clyde, the other, later known as Dere Street, running through the hills from Corbridge on the Tyne past the former command fort at Newstead and on to the Forth. Another road connected Clyde with Forth, and a branch ran north, past modern Stirling, to the old Agricolan legionary fortress at Inchtuthil and beyond. The condition of those roads must have deteriorated since the permanent occupation, especially that north of the Forth-Clyde line, but the others should have been in passable repair, and they offered fast routes into the heart of Scotland, especially for cavalry regiments. Any tactical probe into the area would have the great advantage of a detailed knowledge of camp sites, river crossings and of tracks through the woods and marshes. The years of occupation had not been wasted in that respect, and every unit commander in the frontier zone must have possessed maps of the north, along with a variety of tactical information.

The Wall on the crags to the west of Housesteads.

The Wall above Crag Lough, from the east.

To the north of the Wall there lay outpost forts. Those on Dere Street (Risingham and High Rochester) were apparently not occupied in Hadrian's reign and can be omitted from the discussion at this point, but the western series (Bewcastle, Birrens and Netherby) were held, probably by part-mounted infantry regiments. Immediately in front of the Wall lay the ditch, a formidable obstacle, approximately 30 feet wide and 9 feet deep. The Wall itself ultimately stretched from the north shore of the Tyne near the fort at Wallsend to Bowness on Solway, a distance of 80 Roman miles, or 73 1/2 English miles. At regular intervals close to one Roman mile (1620 yards) small fortlets, with broad gates to north and south, were inserted into the structure, and they housed the patrol garrison. Their regular spacing has rightly given them their modern name of milecastles. In between each pair of milecastles were two turrets, presumably for observation purposes. At less regular intervals there were ultimately 17 forts for auxiliary regiments on or close to the line of the Wall. Linking the forts and milecastles there was a military road, and to the south of that lay a great earthwork, known to us as the Vallum, a wide flat-bottomed ditch with small ramparts set back from both northern and southern lips. A series of turrets and milecastles, known as watch-towers and mile-fortlets to distinguish them from the structures on the Wall itself, stretched down the west coast from the Wall's terminal fort at Bowness to St. Bees Head, a further 40 Roman miles, and three or four support forts supplemented their garrison. On the east coast there was a good port at South Shields, where the vital supplies for the garrison could be landed and stored in safety. South of this complex lay an important series of forts, on the main roads and on the lesser roads, whose tactical role was linked to that of the Wall garrison. Finally, at York and Chester, lay two legions, the strategic reserve. York was the headquarters of the northern command, for the legion at Chester also had responsibilities in Wales.

All these components eventually formed the new frontier system in Britain. Their relationship to each other, and the successive stages of their growth, are not finally resolved, but we know enough to visualise the broad pattern of strategy as it developed. Throughout it must be remembered that Hadrian's Wall and its garrison never stood alone: they were an integral part of a much broader scheme, and without their supporting regiments the troops on the Wall would have been trapped between two fires.

Stone commemorating construction by the Second Legion Augusta.

8

A lonely survivor - the complete milestone on the Stanegate road below Vindolanda.

The Original Plan

Hadrian's blue print in A.D.120 called for a curtain wall, ten Roman feet thick and, it is calculated, fifteen feet high to the rampart walk, from the bridge-head at Newcastle to the river Irthing, and a turf wall, twenty feet wide at the base and perhaps fifteen feet high, from thence to Bowness on Solway. The barrier was to be fronted by a standard V-shaped ditch throughout its length. The total distance of the Wall at this stage was close to 76 Roman miles, of which 45 miles were in stone. It was to be laid out in long straight lengths, without undue regard to variations in ground level, except on the crags on the central sector and alongside the wavering shore of the Solway in the west. No attempt was made to allow minor variations from the straight course in order to take in high ground for tactical purposes. On the crags to the west of Housesteads the Wall took a direct line up the steep slopes and then followed the ridge on the summit, but occasionally, as at Walltown crags, the Wall drops down from the summit a few yards on the northern slope, to give the builders easier foundations. In the west, near Port Carlisle, the Turf Wall and its stone successor ran very close to the water's edge, and the ridge on which it stood was fronted by a salt marsh. There, in places, the army engineers had been forced to lay down an artificial foundation to take the structure, and excavation at Milecastle 79 showed that the lowest level was resting

9

The Wall snaking along the crest of the Whinsill crags at Walltown, near the Roman Army Museum.

The Wall ditch at Limestone Corner, cutting through solid rock before the work was abandoned.

The remains of the latrine building at Housesteads fort. A very modern convenience, if somewhat small for the large garrison.

In the original Turf sector, west of the Irthing, the milecastles were built of turf and timber, in the manner of this replica gateway section at Vindolanda.

on an artificial platform of alternative layers of gravel and earth. This artificial bank may have been necessary to lift the seaward parts above the level of spring and flood tides. In laying down this directive, Hadrian was following his practice in Germany, where his work on Domitian's frontier (limes) involved the straightening out of many sectors of the old line, abandoning the attempt at continuous tactical command over hostile territory. The same consideration affected the positioning of the milecastles, designed to accommodate the patrol garrisons and to offer access to the north, and the observation and signalling turrets between them. With only minor concessions to the military architects, who would have found some of the measured positions impossibly complicated, the milecastles and turrets were not placed with any special regard for high ground or accessibility. There was one clear advantage in such ruthless attachment to symmetry, for the Wall could not create the feeling that it was a defensive barrier which the army would defend.

Cawfields milecastle (no. 42), perched uncomfortably on the whinstone ridge.

Function of the Wall

That the Wall was not designed for defensive fighting is abundantly clear, whatever impression the remains may give. R.G. Collingwood pointed out many years ago that such a view, suggested by Rudyard Kipling in his 'Puck of Pook's Hill', was

11

untenable. If the Wall had been built to stand a siege, both its line and the position of its milecastles would have been very different. But more important, the Roman army was never trained to fight from such a position. The rampart-walk was narrow - perhaps seven or eight feet in the Broad Wall sector and much narrower elsewhere - and access to it could only be gained from the milecastle steps or the turret ladders, all positions over 500 yards apart. Reinforcement of a threatened area would thus be extremely difficult. Nowhere along the line of the Wall were there any catapult positions, and artillery would surely have been of prime importance in a defensive role. The auxiliaries themselves, who were initially stationed to the rear of the Wall, on the Stanegate, possessed few archers, who would have been essential if static defence was the object, but instead consisted of infantrymen and cavalry, in almost equal proportions. The value of cavalry in such a position needs no comment: the role of the auxiliary soldier needs little more. Armed with two throwing spears and a short sword, he could not have contributed very much to defence beyond moral support. His spears were designed to break down his enemy's shield to prepare the way for a sword thrust. If he threw those spears at the enemy below him he could do no more: henceforth his role would be that of an interested spectator.

The milecastle gates betray the true purpose of the Wall. Through any of the 76 gates a Roman force could deploy to the north, having the great advantage of being able to assemble out of sight of the enemy and attack at whatever point seemed best. Battle would be joined, in other words, in normal Roman fashion, out in the country-side to the north of the Wall, where the discipline and training of the auxiliary forces would be felt to advantage. The subsidiary role of the gateways was to allow supervised entry and exit to the province: travellers would be searched for weapons or contra-band, taxed and documented. Perhaps Hadrian felt that this new frontier might even pay for itself one day.

The frontier garrison behind the Wall now had much greater security from the northern barbarians, at any rate. The enemy was split in two: the Brigantians, defeated but not tamed, were denied access to their cousins and allies beyond the Wall, thus preventing concerted action. Free movement between the Pennines and the modern Border hills was effectively halted for the first and only time in British history. All trade was subject to taxation, and it was almost impossible to avoid the customs dues. But the Wall had an important effect upon morale as well.

It marked in unmistakeable manner the limit of the Roman empire. To the north the barbarians were excluded. They might enter into treaty relationships with Rome, receive subsidies and benefit from the Wall markets, but that depended upon good behaviour. To the south the message was even clearer: the Brigantians, whether they liked it or not, were now firmly within the Roman province. There was to be no escape.

The preparation for the work must have created the biggest upheaval in the army of Britain since Agricola's campaigns in Scotland. The legions had to move out of their fortresses, newly converted into imposing stone structures, leaving behind perhaps a skeleton maintenance and administrative staff. Instead they had to construct labour camps in the Tyne-Solway gap, where for the greater part of the year they would have to live in their leather tents and spend their days in the quarries or in the production line from them to the Wall itself. Administrative staff and the centurions probably found more comfortable quarters in the nearby auxiliary forts. Recent excavation at Vindolanda has revealed the presence of legionary officers at this time, heavily preoccupied with the acquisition of supplies for their men. The villages and towns near the fortresses must have felt the economic draught, although it is presumed that the troops would return during the winter months. New docking facilities would have to be constructed both on the Tyne and in the Solway, and requisition orders would be required to increase the available transport. What the Brigantians and the inhabitants of southern Scotland thought of these preparations is not difficult to imagine, and a very careful watch would have to be maintained over them by the auxiliary troops.

Wall building 1970's style, with pupils of Heathfield Senior High School, Gateshead, at Vindolanda.

The Work Schedule for the Legions

Our knowledge of the Wall has progressed so rapidly in the past 50 years that it is now possible to see the glimmerings of the actual work-plan as the legions were assigned to their various tasks. Stones recording work on the structures completed by legions, cohorts and centuries have been found amongst the tumble from the ruins or still in position in the Wall (although, unfortunately, the quality of these stones does not compare with those later built into the Antonine Wall in Scotland), and a careful analysis of their positions has been used to calculate the amount of work assigned to each legion. The matter is complicated by the lack of precise information about the findspot of many of the stones, and the promotion of centurions within the legion, or their transfer to a different legion, may upset calculations on the disposition of the individual cohorts during the work. Even more confusing is the knowledge that some of the inscriptions were left by units which later took part in re-building operations, and not all their stones record that such reconstruction was taking place.

Hadrianic building inscription from milecastle 38, naming
Platorius Nepos as Governor of Britain.

14

The Strength of the Construction Force

Before examining the construction work in greater detail, we must first assess the strength of the force available. As far as we know, the building was the work of the legions alone, perhaps because only they had the necessary skills to accomplish the task. Auxiliaries undoubtedly assisted them on tasks within their powers, such as digging ditches and carrying stone, and even the marines from the fleet were enrolled at one point. Native labour may have been used sparingly, but it was likely to cause more trouble than it was worth. Unfortunately, it is at this point in the history of Roman Britain that we lack essential information about the strength of the legions.

The replica sections of Wall at Vindolanda, completed in 1973.

II Augusta from Caerleon and the XX Valeria Victrix from Chester were both available for construction work, and numerous records of their activity on the Wall have been found. We also know that VI Victrix was brought to Britain probably in A.D.122, perhaps accompanying the new governor, Platorius Nepos, and its building inscriptions are also plentiful. What had become of IX Hispana? The controversy is an old one, and in spite of recent evidence, the legend of its annihilation dies hard. But Eric Birley pointed out as long ago as 1948 that such a view is most unlikely, and since then further evidence has come to light to preserve the Ninth's reputation. It now

15

seems likely that it was withdrawn from Britain, either before Wall building commenced or soon afterwards, and that its fate is the concern of another province, probably in the East.

The Vallum ditch cut through the solid rock near Limestone Corner.

As the legions prepared their temporary work camps - the normal marching camp, with ditch and rampart with a timber palisade upon it, but with perhaps some timber buildings in the interior in place of the customary leather tents - and while the legionary generals discussed their allocations of sectors with their centurions, the most common attitude must have been one of awe, mingled with apprehension. The task was colossal, even for the skilled legionary craftsmen. The Wall was to be ten Roman feet thick in the stone sector, and the height to the rampart-walk must have been approximately fifteen Roman feet. Today its highest portion is not more than ten feet, but antiquaries have recorded much more substantial sections in their day. One of the minor tragedies of British history is that the Venerable Bede did not record its surviving dimensions accurately. He wrote at the monastery of Monkwearmouth and Jarrow, just across the Tyne from the Wall, and there is little doubt that he must have seen its ruins himself, whilst some of his brother monks had no doubt searched the old fort-sites for building stones. The Latin inscriptions must have tempted one or two of the monks to pause a while in their labours. Christopher Ridley, curate of Haltwhistle, recorded c 1572 heights of 21 feet in places, whilst Edward Threkald, chancellor of the diocese of Hereford but born and bred at Burgh by Sands, informed Camden in 1574 that the Wall stood sixteen feet high near Bowness. However, the dimensions of the Wall ditch probably give as good a guide to the height of the Wall as anything. It must have been possible for a sentry on the rampart-walk to see the bottom of the ditch, otherwise it could become a useful hiding place for infiltrators, and calculations based upon such an assumption produce a figure of 15 Roman feet for the height of the rampart-walk above ground level, and a parapet on the northern face might have added a further five feet or so to that figure. Thus the 45 miles of stone-wall called for in the original plan would have required some two million tons of stone, quarried and shaped with crossbars and chisels. Lime for the mortar was also needed in vast quantities, and special provision would have to be made to carry water to the masons working on the Wall face.

Roman legionaries ponder the tasks ahead - as portrayed by the Ermine Street Guard.

Very little research has been devoted to the source of these quarries, but the situation of some is well known. On Fallowfield fell, east of Chollerford, the words '(P)etra Flavi Caranti' were carved on the rock-face, where Flavius Carantus put his name to the section he was working. Some quarries were inevitably a distance from the Wall. On Barcombe, the steep heather-clad hill to the south-west of Housesteads, there was another Wall quarry, and when it was re-opened in 1837 one of the workers,

17

Thomas Pattinson from Haltwhistle, found a mouldering bronze arm-purse, containing 3 gold coins and 60 silver coins. All the coins were current in the reign of Hadrian, and although the near-by fort of Vindolanda was occupied at this time, the purse may have belonged to a soldier engaged on Wall construction. Investigation of these quarries should prove rewarding, for there are many variants of sandstone in the area, and in some cases it should be possible to identify the quarry from which certain building stones had been cut. But it must be remembered that quarrying and lime burning were once major industries in the area near the central sector of the Wall, and many of the worked rock faces have no connection with the Romans.

The Turf Wall, 31 Roman miles long, did not present such formidable difficulties, but its construction was no easy task. To build it, 20-25 feet wide at base and some 12-15 feet high, a strip of ground at least 80 yards deep would have to be denuded of turf, and the turves cut by the Roman army were massive, a regulation 18" by 12" and 6" deep. The Turf Wall would have been crowned with a timber parapet, but although it would not look as impressive as its stone counterpart, it would be just as effective.

There may still be room for argument about the allocation of Wall lengths to the legions, and about the number of cohorts which actually worked on the face, but there is no doubt that the work was carried out magnificently. The rectangular facing stones were mortared to form an unclimbable and indestructable cliff, and with a core of broken rubble, onto which liquid mortar had been poured at intervals of every eighteen inches or so, the Wall would stand without further maintenance until the weather ultimately weakened the mortar. Only then would the natives have a chance of destroying it.

The Milecastles

The Milecastles have significant variations in design which are attributable to the different legions which built them, but their internal lay-out is similar. Each contained one or two barrack buildings, to house a garrison of from 25 to 50 men, and in a corner of the structure a field oven would be used for baking bread. A flight of steps gave access to the rampart-walk. The two great gateways, to the north and south, enabled the swift passage of auxiliary battalions and their baggage carts through the barrier, and ensured that natives would go through the full passport procedure before entering or leaving the province. Each milecastle was presumably linked to the turrets on either side of it, and the garrison thus had extra accommodation. There are no external buildings outside the milecastles, which provides a firm clue to the nature of the garrison, as will be seen, and the evidence of ditches, traced outside milecastles 23, 25, 29 & 51, has yet to be tested by excavation.

It is clear that the construction gangs responsible for the milecastles (and turrets) were working ahead of the curtain builders in the central sector, for west of milecastle 27, where the Wall was never built to its ten Roman feet, although a foundation for

The remains of the later blocking wall inside the north gate of Milecastle 37.

Excavation of Turret 7B, 1930's style.

such a structure had been laid, the milecastle gateway had already been constructed and provided with wing walls to balance the structures until they could be bonded into the Wall when the builders reached them. But by the time the builders arrived, they were building narrow wall, and at each junction with milecastle wing walls an untidy reduction point betrayed the change in plan.

Only one of the turf milecastles in the western sector has survived, (50 TW), in that small loop whose course was not followed by the later stone-wall builders. But it seems that their walls were of turf and clay, with a timber palisade, and that the internal arrangements were similar to those of the stone milecastles in the east.

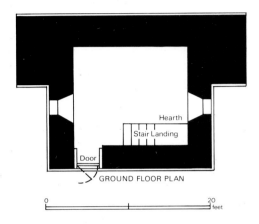

Ground plan of an observation turret.

Turrets

Between each pair of milecastles there were two turrets, constructed in stone at once throughout the length of the Wall. They were fourteen feet square internally, and were designed primarily for observation and signalling purposes, but they could also accommodate a small detachment of men, and they appear to have been regularly inhabited. Like the milecastles, they were built in advance of the curtain gangs, and their wing walls exhibit the same untidy bonding joints. In the western sector they naturally did not have wing walls of stone, and the turf rampart was laid against their walls.

The turrets had an upper storey above the rampart walk, and their height was probably close to 30 feet - at any rate in the Broad Wall sector. When the curtain wall was lower, there may have been a similar reduction in the height of the turrets. The excavated turrets demonstrate that their doors opened outwards, on the southern side, and that the lofty ground floor rooms had windows in eastern and western walls, to let in the light and to let out the smoke from the hearths. The roofs seem to have been of slate. Insufficient excavation has been attempted to assign the turrets firmly to the different legions, but it is reasonable to assume that the milecastle builders were responsible for the turrets on either side.

The Garrison of the Milecastles & Turrets

There has been considerable speculation about the nature of the milecastle and turret garrisons, for we lack both literary and epigraphic evidence. There is provision for a patrol force of some 2,500 men, but it seems clear that they were neither auxiliary soldiers nor the less well trained numeri, who do not appear to have served in Britain until the third century. The administrative problems entailed in splitting auxiliary units into groups of 25 and 50 men, and allocating them to the separated fortlets would have been excessive, and it would have destroyed the effectiveness of that unit in battle. Numeri are not known to have been enlisted into the Roman army in Britain, until the third century, and there is no record of their presence on the Wall until that date. Archaeological evidence points to a much lower standard of living in the milecastles than in the forts nearby, and it has so far failed to reveal any trace of extra-mural buildings, such as bath-houses, shops, inns or ordinary houses. This must provide an important clue to the nature of the garrisons, for it is inconceivable that Hadrian should neglect or bar the presence of such necessary amenities when he was so passionately concerned about the morale of his troops. Without the normal amenities, the life of the milecastle garrisons must have been dreary in the extreme, and it seems, therefore, that the men cannnot have been permanently stationed there. It is much more likely that they were on short-service duty on the frontier, for perhaps a few months at a time, and involved in nothing more important than patrol and customs duties. Such a force is possibly to be associated with the new Romano-British farm-steads which sprang up at this time in the valley to the north of the Wall.

Selected plots of land would be given to reliable natives - not necessarily British, perhaps German or Raetian - on the condition that in rotation they did duty on the Wall. Such a scheme would have many attractions. The farmstead, protected by cavalry patrols, would cultivate an otherwise deserted area and act as a buffer against hostile aggression from the north, while the cattle from the farms would feed the northern garrison. The contact that their service in the milecastles would give these men would gradually create a body of reservists, to be enlisted, not necessarily unwillingly, in the auxiliary regiments in an emergency.

The Bridges

Two important aspects of the original plan remain to be mentioned. The Wall had to cross three major rivers on its course across the country - the North Tyne, the

The Wall bridge crossing the North Tyne, with Chesters fort bath house on the river bank.

Irthing and the Eden, besides a number of lesser streams such as the Haltwhistle Burn, the Poltross Burn and the Cambeck. Bridging of some kind would be required at all such crossings. At the North Tyne crossing opposite Chesters fort, the first Hadrianic bridge was designed, as at the crossing of the Irthing at Willowford, to carry the Wall alone. It had cutwaters on its piers both up and down stream, and the superstructure lay above great stone arches. There were signs that gratings or chains may have been slung beneath the arches, to prevent unauthorised passage down the river. The major bridge at Newcastle, Pons Aelius, must have been constructed at this time as well, since its presence was essential to the Wall builders and to the garrison. Its construction was probably the greatest engineering feat of all, and the discovery of two altars, perhaps from a bridgehead shrine, dedicated to Neptune and to Ocean by the Sixth Legion, suggest that the new legion was employed upon this task as soon as it arrived.

The Wall Ditch

Finally there was a great V-shaped ditch to the north of the Wall. The berm or space between the northern face of the Wall and the southern lip of the ditch was twenty feet in the stone Wall sector and only six feet in the turf sector, but the width and depth of the ditch varied according to the nature of the subsoil. At Heddon, cut in rock, it is 34 feet wide and nearly 9 feet deep; on the Carvoran to Thirlwall bank it is nearly 40 feet wide and 10 feet deep; but the norm was close to that at Chesters and Housesteads, where it has been found to be 27 feet wide and 9 feet deep. In shape it was a standard military ditch, with sharply sloping sides and small square drainage channel running along the bottom. The upcast from the ditch was spread out on the north lip, sloping gently away as to afford an enemy no cover. In certain stretches the ditch was never cut, due to the presence of crags which rendered it superfluous, and in other sectors it had been left unfinished for some reason.

The forts are added to the Wall, as here at Housesteads.

Thus at Limestone Corner one can see the progress of the ditch gang before it was suddenly interrupted. The men had been working eastwards, past the front of milecastle 30. A length of ditch was nearly finished and another 50 yard stretch had been largely dug, although blocks of whinstone still remained on the ditch bottom, ready for splitting and lifting out. In the next stretch the topsoil had been removed, but the rock had not been touched. Perhaps it was the end of the season, and the gangs never returned, or perhaps some sensible commanding officer decided that it was hardly worth the trouble involved to cut through such rock. At any rate, the section survives today and gives a vivid impression of the huge task that those Roman soldiers had been forced to tackle. Recent experience (the construction of replica stretches at

23

Vindolanda) has reminded us that ditch digging was probably the hardest if not the most expensive of all the construction tasks involved in the new frontier. Turf digging and carrying are monotonous but not over-strenuous occupations, and wall building, though exhausting, is at least varied and satisfying. Ditch digging through swamp, boulder clay and rock, is immensely arduous and soul-destroying, even in good weather. If it rains, the task is almost impossible. Tens of thousands of visitors today look at the remains of the stone Wall and respect the men who once fashioned it, but few honour those who dug the ditch. It was, perhaps, the task of the auxiliaries.

Rather more than half the Wall had been built before the original plan was changed.

Wall Building: Amended Plan:
The Addition of the Forts and the Vallum

Archaeological evidence has demonstrated that the new frontier, although the work of Hadrian, was not constructed at one time, nor were some features planned at all when the curtain wall builders started. It is not yet possible to fit all of the additions into a firm time-scale, but the major alterations are clear, and the Vallum has produced the vital evidence.

In the first place, a section cut through the Vallum in Wall-mile 11/12 showed that the prominent mounds, or ramparts, set back on each side of the ditch were composed of material dug from the ditch, and thus are both contemporary with that ditch. There could be no question, therefore, that the Vallum had originally faced north only and had thus stood as an independent frontier line. Then it was shown that the Vallum ditch made a southward and symetrical diversion round some of the Wall forts, which proved that the forts were at least planned before the Vallum was dug. The course of the Vallum was interrupted by an original stone-revetted roadway almost twenty feet wide opposite Birdoswald fort, and this roadway was spanned by an arched gateway of massive ashlar blocks, although it had been largely demolished in the Roman period.

Excavation at Benwell added a further example of such a causeway and the remains of the gateway were sufficiently preserved to show that its large double gate had been opened and closed from the north, thus proving that the Vallum was controlled from north not south. Since then similar causeways have been found opposite both Housesteads and Greatchesters, but in neither case were there any remains of the gateway.

Haltonchesters was one of the Wall forts which the Vallum carefully avoided by a diversion. Excavation revealed that the fort lay astride the Wall itself, and that its construction had entailed the removal of Wall foundation and the filling in of the Wall ditch. Haltonchesters was thus secondary to the Wall - and the Vallum was not built before the fort was at least planned.

24

At Carrawburgh, a late fort which was only built during the governorship of Sextus Julius Severus (130-132) the Vallum was found to underlie the fort, and it had been methodically filled in when the fort builders levelled the site before construction began. Thus although the Vallum was later than the Wall and not earlier than the original forts, it was nevertheless an integral part of the Hadrianic frontier system.

It is not yet clear whether there were originally causeways over the Vallum opposite the milecastles. The evidence from Milecastles 50 and 51 on the Turf Wall, and the visible signs opposite the milecastle at Limestone Corner suggest that there were original causeways, but excavation at other points has found no trace. Any crossings additional to those opposite the forts would place a greater strain upon the milecastle garrisons and would reduce the effectiveness of the Vallum itself, and there may thus be special reasons for a limited number only. Only further excavation can solve this problem. Milecastle garrisons would cross the ditch easily enough if they possessed a portable wooden bridge, normally stored on the north berm.

The remains of the gated Vallum crossing to the south of Benwell fort.

It is impossible to judge whether the modifications to the original plan, which together altered the whole concept of the Wall, were conceived at one time, or whether there was more than one change of plan. It looks as though the decision to add eleven forts to the Wall and to construct the Vallum behind them was simultaneous, although there could have been a slight time lag. Carrawburgh, and probably Drumburgh, were

25

not planned until a little later. The three outpost forts in the west, Bewcastle, Birrens and Netherby, are all Hadrianic and would seem to be an essential part of the plan. Inscriptions from Birrens and Netherby show that they were under construction before Hadrian took the title of Father of his Country (Pater Patriae), in A.D.128, and Bewcastle would appear to be essential once a decision to have such forts north of the Wall had been taken.

The milecastle, turret and supporting fort system down the Cumberland coast is as yet undated, but by inference it should belong to the same period as the 4 mile eastern extension to Wallsend, although it might be part of the original plan. In sum, however, the changes produced a much more carefully defined frontier, with a narrow military zone stretching continuously across the country, accessible from both north and south only at controlled crossings, and with greater flank protection than that included in the original scheme. Experience eventually demanded one further addition to these installations, and a military road was to be laid down behind the Wall, linking the forts and milecastles: the Vallum had rendered the position of the Stanegate too awkward for daily use by the Wall garrison.

It is impossible to be certain of the reason for these changes. It has been argued that they may have been anticipated. Some of the alterations, if not all, may have stemmed from the brain of the Emperor himself. He was an acknowledged expert in military matters, and he was usually at pains to demonstrate his architectural ability as well. If he inspected the great frontier works and found no fault, it would imply that he could not improve upon them, and the breadth of the changes, involving a major increase in the construction load, suggests that the Emperor was demonstrating his own superiority.

The extra burden upon the legions was very real. The digging of the Vallum ditch was a comparatively straightforward task, in spite of the difficulties presented by solid rock and dangerous bogs and much of it could be delegated to the auxiliaries, but the addition of the forts was another matter. They alone demanded additional reinforcements to the British legions, and they should explain the arrival of the Sixth Legion in the province in A.D.122. It is impossible, at the moment, to be certain about the timing of the three important arrivals of that year. By July Britain had welcomed a new governor, Aulus Platorius Nepos, an old friend of the Emperor, and in the same year Hadrian himself had visited Britain for the first and only time in his reign. We can only speculate until a fresh inscription or diploma throws light on the problem. But it would seem logical to suppose that the retiring governor, Pompeius Falco, had reported to Hadrian personally on the progress of the frontier works, perhaps while he was on the Rhine, inspecting the army in Germany. Hadrian perhaps accompanied the new governor to Britain in the summer of 122 and together they inspected the situation for themselves. The change of plan demanded further legionary troops if the construction of the forts was to be completed in a reasonable time, and Nepos requested the Sixth Legion from his former province. It could have disembarked on the Tyne in the late autumn of 122, to be thoroughly briefed and prepared for its task

The massive granaries at Corbridge.

before the opening of the building season in 123.

The new plan scrapped the Stanegate fort system and moved a heavier concentration of troops up to the Wall itself. It gave the units greater scope for operations to the north of the Wall, but of more immediate importance the creation of the Vallum was to protect them from any southerly sorties as well. Hadrian disliked the growth of sprawling villages outside the forts: the beer-houses and theatres distracted the troops and led to slackness and poor morale, and such dangers were minimised by the new scheme which debarred civilians from the entire military zone. Army stores and live-stock were now protected, and military troop movements along the line of the Wall would not be hindered in any way by crowds of camp-followers or idle natives. It was a tidy and efficient arrangement.

The Forts

The combined evidence of the Notitia, the Rudge Cup and the Amiens skillet and surviving structures gives us seventeen forts that can be described as being 'per lineam Valli'. Two of these, Vindolanda, nearly a mile south of the Wall and Crag Lough in the central sector, and Carvoran near Greenhead were old Stanegate forts. The other

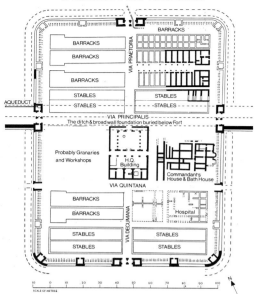

A CAVALRY FORT (CHESTERS)

BARRACKS

BARRACKS

BARRACKS

VIA PRAETORIA

BARRACKS

BARRACKS

BARRACKS

STABLES

STABLES

STABLES

STABLES

AQUEDUCT

VIA PRINCIPALIS
The ditch & broad wall foundation buried below Fort

Probably Granaries
and Workshops

H.Q.
Building

Commandant's
House & Bath House

VIA QUINTANA

BARRACKS

BARRACKS

VIA DECUMANA

Hospital

STABLES

STABLES

STABLES

STABLES

10   0   10   20   30   40   50   60   70   80   90   100
SCALE OF METRES

Plan of a cavalry fort.

15 were spaced, without any immediately obvious regard for regularity, along the line of the Wall, or very close to it, at intervals ranging from nearly nine miles (Castlesteads to Stanwix) to three miles (Carvoran to Greatchesters and Carvoran to Birdoswald). Excavation has however demonstrated that not all these forts are original, and the elimination of the secondary group (Wallsend, probably Newcastle, Carrawburgh, Carvoran and Drumburgh) reveals a planned spacing for the original eleven forts. It is assumed that Greatchesters was planned in the original scheme although the evidence suggests that it was not completed until c.130, perhaps because its function could be adequately covered by the nearby Stanegate fort at Carvoran, until more urgent building had been completed. Its position in the original scheme is virtually assured by the discovery of a Vallum crossing opposite the fort.

A study of plans of these primary forts, together with the little knowledge that we have of the Hadrianic garrisons, points to an equally schematic arrangement of garrisons. Housesteads, Greatchesters, Birdoswald and Castlesteads were planned to house infantry battalions amounting to a brigade of some 4,000 strong. On either flank lay cavalry brigades, 2,000 strong: in the west Stanwix, Burgh by Sands and Bowness, and in the east Benwell, Rudchester, Haltonchesters and Chesters. Stanwix was the key fort in the system, for it housed a cavalry regiment 1,000 strong, the only unit of its kind in the army of Britain, and its commanding officer was the senior officer in the Wall zone.

28

The west gate at Housesteads fort, with the later blocking walls removed.

The revision of the plan which transferred the auxiliaries to the Wall itself necessitated a considerable increase in the volume of construction work. Some effort to compensate for this can be seen in the decision to reduce the width of the curtain wall, in the sections not yet built, to 8 Roman feet instead of 10. It may be that the height of the Wall was correspondingly reduced, perhaps to 12 Roman feet, unless such a reduction created problems at the junctions with the turrets and milecastles, which had already been constructed to the larger scale. But if the height was not lowered, there would nevertheless be a major saving in the amount of rubble core and mortar necessary for the space between the facing stones. The revised scale resulted in a change from Milecastle 27 westwards to the Irthing, and there the narrower Wall stands on, or alongside (west of Greatchesters) the already prepared broad foundation. On the Whin Sill crags in the central sector, the width may have been reduced to as little as six feet, with a corresponding reduction in height, for here the Wall was virtually superfluous.

Collingwood Bruce in the nineteenth century attempted some calculations designed to estimate the work-load of the legions in the construction of the new frontier. Assuming a height of 16 feet for the Wall and a uniform thickness of 8 feet, he reckoned that each cubic yard of Wall would require, in quarrying stone, carrying it to

The foundations of the north gate at Housesteads, after the roadway had been removed.

the Wall, setting it in place, etc., one full day's work for one man. Judging by modern standards his reckoning was wildly optimistic, but even so the stone Wall would require 1,702,115 days of man labour. These calculations took no account of the additional work required for milecastles, turrets and forts, and his figure perhaps needs doubling when they are included. The ditch to the north of the Wall was, of course, a more simple task, but it nevertheless involved the removal of over $5\frac{1}{2}$ million cubic yards of earth and stone. Bruce felt that a hard-working labourer of his own day, with suitable incentives, and with modern equipment, might shift 20 cubic yards a day, but he assumed, probably incorrectly, that unwilling and ill-fed natives would be forced to do the work by Roman overseers, and that 8 cubic yards a day was all that could be expected from them. This would necessitate nearly 700,000 days labour for one man. On the same basis, the Vallum would require some 465,000 days of labour. Such calculations are no more than vague indications of the task that the Romans faced, and some would doubt whether the Vallum would require less labour than the ditch to the north of the Wall, since its construction involved the careful building of the symmetrical banks of earth or ramparts, on both sides of the ditch, together with great gates at the causeway crossings. It would be worthwhile for someone to attempt a fresh appraisal of the work load in the light of modern research on the frontier. Obviously there are many unknown factors in the construction scheme. We know

*The north gate at Housesteads, with the Wall heading east towards
Sewing Shields Crags.*

*The headquarters building of the Fourth Cohort of Gauls,
at Vindolanda.*

31

nothing of the degree of which forced labour was enrolled, nor do we know the involvement of the auxiliary troops. A substantial number of men must have been swallowed up in administrative or commissariat tasks, and others might have to stand guard over the builders. We would also have to guess at the availability of transport to carry the stones from the quarries to the working-face and for the amount of lime required for mortar, but such an attempt might allow us to have a closer insight into the construction of the frontier.

The reduction in size of the Wall certainly saved the legionary masons from the laborious task of cutting several thousand tons of stone, and with a correspondingly smaller demand upon waggon transport, the whole work could be accelerated. But the decision to add stone forts for the garrison more than made up for this saving. With perhaps 16 or 17 new forts (including outposts) to be built, the army commissariat had to produce a huge quantity of fresh building materials. The faced stones and rubble for the fort walls and internal building walls could presumably be cut from the quarries already in use. The clay, essential for levelling the fort sites, could also be dug from the subsoil close to the working areas. But great stockpiles of seasoned timber would have to be built up ready for the legionary joiners, together with clay roofing tiles, or stone slates, lead for pipes and water-tank joints, iron nails of all sizes by the ton, and huge quantities of lime for the plastering. And whereas comparatively raw legionaries could, with a little training, be safely entrusted with the construction of the curtain wall, more experienced men would be required for the fort buildings and installations. There is little doubt that the Sixth Legion was earmarked for this fresh work.

While the bulk of the legionary troops concentrated on the construction of forts and Wall, others began to drive the massive earthwork of the Vallum through rock and swamp from the banks of the Tyne at Newcastle to the sea at Bowness. Although a much less costly operation than the construction of the forts, it was still a considerable undertaking and one must presume that several auxiliary battalions were enrolled into its labour force.

The course of the Vallum is known to diverge opposite the forts of Benwell, Haltonchesters, Carvoran, Birdoswald and Castlesteads, and it must be presumed to have done the same at Rudchester, Chesters, Stanwix and Burgh by Sands. The ditch was never cut out at the crossings opposite the forts at Benwell, Housesteads, Birdoswald and Greatchesters, which proves that the fort positions had at least been marked out, if building had not already started, when the Vallum diggers reached them. We know from Carrawburgh, the late addition to the fort scheme added c130-132, that the Vallum was already dug before the fort builders reached the site, and it is probably best to regard the decision to add the Vallum as simultaneous with that to add the first forts. Indeed, the forts can hardly have been contemplated after the Vallum work had begun, since its presence would be a major inconvenience to the regiments stationed to the south of it.

A standard section of the Vallum would reveal a ditch twenty feet wide at the

A long sweep of the Vallum, to the east of Cawfields.

top and eight feet wide across the flat bottom, ten feet deep and with sides sloping at 60 degrees. Where significant variations occur, such as east of milecastle 42, where the ditch was 34 feet wide, 4 feet across the bottom, $10\frac{1}{2}$ feet deep and with sides sloping at 35 degrees, they are normally taken to represent re-cuttings at a later date. The upcast from the ditch was placed symmetrically in mounds on either side of the ditch, set back some 30 feet from the lip. These 20 feet wide mounds were sometimes revetted with kerbs of turfwork, to ensure that they stood up sharply, but this was not general practice. There are many minor variations in the dimensions, which demonstrates that the army surveyors took account of the varying subsoil along its course, and modified their plans accordingly. Where the subsoil permitted, the ditch was steep-sided, as through the hard rock of Limestone Corner or through the boulder clay at Benwell, but where conditions were less stable much shallower slopes had to be created. The consistent features were the flat bottom of the ditch, which was very different to standard military practice, the north and south mounds, and an overall measurement from north to south of approximately 120 feet.

The earthwork was laid out across the country like a Roman road, normally close to the Wall, but sometimes as much as half a mile to the south of it. Its course ignored good tactical ground, and where it clung to the lower slopes of a valley, as to the west of Housesteads, it would have been a hopeless position to defend, or to view

The massive remains of the south pier of the bridge which carried the Wall across the North Tyne at Chesters.

The East Gate of Birdoswald fort, the best preserved example on the Wall.

34

the country to the south. Unlike the ditch to the north of the Wall, it was continuous across the Tyne-Solway ithsmus, and this is particularly emphasised by its cut through the rock at Limestone Corner, the very point at which the ditch-diggers to the north of the Wall ultimately abandoned their task.

Opposite some of the milecastles there are causeways, but these are not necessarily original work, and there has as yet been insufficient excavation to be certain of the position in the original scheme. The work at Turf Wall milecastles 50 and 51 suggested there had been original causeways there, but there was no sign of such crossings at milecastles 23, 30 and 42. If there were causeways opposite the milecastles in the original plan, their presence would place a much greater strain upon the garrison, and they were hardly necessary for patrol work. Where a patrol needed to cross a ditch, a portable wooden bridge would be sufficient for their needs, and such an aid could have been stored on the north berm of the ditch, opposite the milecastle, ready for use.

The existence of the Vallum thus had a two-fold purpose. It protected the military stores and herds of the fort garrison, and it acted as a serious deterrent to raiding parties attempting to cross the frontier from the south. Individuals might cross with little trouble, but they would have to leave their horses and baggage behind.

The Extension to Wallsend

The date of the decision to add forts and Vallum to the Wall was perhaps A.D.122, as has been argued above. It may be that the remaining alterations were planned at the same time. The four mile eastern extension of the Wall from the bridge-head at Newcastle (Pons Aelius) to modern Wallsend was built to an eight foot gauge, without any broad foundation underneath. The reason for such an addition is not clear. It can hardly have affected unauthorised crossing of the Tyne, since the lowest ford was above Newcastle, and any crossing to the east would have to be by boat, in which case the addition of only four more miles of Wall would make little impact. Perhaps Hadrian felt that it was dangerous to end the Wall at the bridge-head since such an important site would be more likely to attract enemy attention than any other, and the extension to Wallsend would give flank protection. The new fort at Wallsend was designed to hold an infantry battalion, unlike its immediate neighbours to the west, and the troops were thus perhaps the only footsoldiers in the region. With their backs to the Tyne and with an apparently peaceful and comparatively prosperous agricultural community in front of them, their duties cannot have involved them in the defensive role of the eastern cavalry brigade. Action, if it came, would probably be against sea-borne raiders. We know little of the fort at Newcastle itself. It was an obvious site, but the duties of its garrison would be confined to the guarding and maintenance of the great bridge, together with the quays on the north banks of the Tyne. If there was a road leading north from Newcastle to link up with the so-called 'Devil's Causeway', they and their fellows at Wallsend might have been expected to send patrols up to Learchild.

A pair of cavalry barracks at Chesters.

The Extension down the Cumbrian Coast

The forty mile Cumbrian coast extension has received more attention in recent years. It will be some years before we can be positive about the date and history of the structures, and there is evidence that they suffered much the same changes in conception and planning and alteration during the course of construction as did those on the Wall. However, there appear to be milefortlets and watch-towers stretching down the west coast from the Wall terminal at Bowness to St. Bees Head, spaced as accurately as those on the Wall itself. A connecting Wall, or frontal ditch, was unnecessary here, but the milefortlets were instead protected by ditches, and forts at Beckfoot, itself on the edge of the shore, Maryport, Burrow Walls and Moresby give more than moral support to the garrison. Finds from the excavations have so far not included an inscription, but at most sites the only pottery to appear has been Hadrianic, and the system is definitely a part of the new frontier complex. It is conceivable that the idea of this coastal watch was a part of the original Hadrianic plan, since the Cumberland coast was an obvious target for sea-raiders from both Ireland and south-west Scotland.

Reconstruction drawing of a typical milecastle.

Some scholars have in the past postulated a similar scheme for the Durham and North Yorkshire coast in the east, but aerial photography and ground excavation have produced nothing to support the idea. There was less likelihood of trouble from the sea in the east during the second century, and it is more likely that the late fourth century fortlets and signal posts were the only ones to be built in that area. The full length of the Hadrianic system was thus almost 120 Roman miles, garrisoned by both a patrol and customs force and by a ready army of auxiliary soldiers.

The conversion of the Turf Wall sector between the Irthing and milecastle 54 took place well before the conversion of the remainder, and it is likely that it was accomplished during this second phase, when stone supplies and mortar had to be taken to Birdoswald fort.

The Outpost Forts

The three outpost forts at Bewcastle, Birrens and Netherby were definitely Hadrianic. The latter two have produced inscriptions confirming that they were constructed before A.D.128, and all three were probably planned from the first, perhaps in the original Wall plan. Their presence in the western sector - and the absence of such advanced forts further east - was predictable. With Stanwix chosen as the base for the most hard-hitting and valuable auxiliary regiment in Britain, it was clear that if trouble was to come, it could be found in the west. There may be several reasons for this. One theory maintains that the sprawling Brigantian confederacy included lands to the north of Carlisle, and the Wall thus bisected a tribal group. Two results might emerge from this. If the Brigantians had at this time come to some sort of terms with Rome, they would surely expect their north-western cousins to be protected by Roman arms from the possible aggression of Novantae and Selgovae: on the other hand, if the Brigantians were still hostile, which is more likely, there would be anger and resentment in the western sector, stemming from groups on both sides of the barrier. There may also have been a heavier concentration of population in the western sector - after all, there can have been comparatively few natives to the north of the Wall in the central sector, since even today with modern drainage and other facilities it is still a wild and uncomfortable region, with an undue proportion of marshland. In the east the Votadini appear to have had a long record of peaceful co-existence with Rome, and forts would not be necessary in their territory, most of which could be patrolled comfortably by the cavalry regiments on the Wall.

A horseman approaches a fort gateway.

38

Whether or not Annandale and Clydesdale were already being affected by a movement of people from Ireland, there was sufficient work to keep the garrisons of Netherby, Birrens and Bewcastle busy. The steep valleys and moors, probably heavily wooded, afforded excellent cover for hostile natives, and the territory must have needed constant vigilance.

Bewcastle was particularly vulnerable, watching over a bleak and exposed countryside, later to be the hunting ground for Border outlaws. But if these outposts could not deal with a determined attack, they could at least give early warning to the Wall headquarters at Stanwix, and a cavalry brigade could sweep into the danger zone within hours.

The insertion of a fort at Carrawburgh, soon after 128, split up the inconveniently long sector between Housesteads and Chesters, which had been caused by the necessity for placing Chesters a mile to the east of its calculated position, in order to guard the Wall crossing of the North Tyne. Designed from the first as an infantry fort, it boosted the strength of the forces in the central sector to some 4,500 men. Similarly, the decision to retain the Stanegate fort at Carvoran in the Wall series was based upon strategic grounds, for it was ideally placed to control the Tipalt Burn gap, whilst Vindolanda, the former Flavian & Trajanic site, watched over the deep valley of the Bradley Burn and the moors to the south of the South Tyne. Finally, the addition of Drumburgh in the west added an infantry unit to a garrison that was otherwise entirely cavalry, and provided therefore the same kind of reinforcement that Wallsend gave in the east.

The New Frontier in Operation

By 132 at any rate, the new frontier was largely complete, and it was physically very different from the original conception of A.D.120, although its purpose had not changed. By now, of course, the emperor himself had probably lost all interest in his scheme, since more serious matters engaged his mind in the East, but he could have taken pride in the technical achievements of his British army. To the natives the sight of the frontier works, whether viewed from the north or from the south, must have been overpowering. An unscalable cliff had been stretched across the country, with ditches in front and behind, and a massive striking force lay restlessly within its bounds, awaiting the opportunity for action.

Although we cannot be certain whether the forts actually held the garrisons for which they were designed, it is reasonable to infer that for a while at any rate they did so. And with such knowledge we can begin to analyse the tactical use of the new Hadrianic frontier. The eastern sector had the advantage of a friendly tribe in front of it. The infantry regiments at Wallsend and Newcastle could effectively police the northern banks of the Tyne and deal with minor local disturbances. Ferries, manned by both Newcastle and South Shields garrisons, would supplement the bridge and ensure a steady flow of supplies westwards. The four cavalry regiments lying at Benwell,

A Roman cavalryman, from the Roman Army Museum.

Rudchester, Haltonchesters and Chesters, along 21 miles of Wall, controlled both the eastern Northumbrian plain and also the northern end of Dere Street. Since the southern approaches to the Wall were already garrisoned by regiments at Chester-le-Street and Binchester, this eastern cavalry brigade was free to concentrate upon a broad tactical role north of the Wall. There would be little chance of cavalry action near the Wall itself: control of the roads and the nature of the countryside would allow daily patrols up to thirty miles north of the Wall, and intelligence reports from frontier scouts could send the full brigade into action in the Forth-Clyde gap within 48 hours. No normal native force could withstand the shock of 2,000 Roman cavalry, and it would be a major emergency indeed if further reinforcements had to be called up.

In the central sector, watching over the forested and marshy highlands, where no cavalry could operate successfully - and this was still true in the late 16th century, as more than one Warden of the Middle March discovered to his cost - the Romans placed their brigades of infantry and part-mounted infantry. Some 4,000 troops, from Housesteads, Greatchesters, Birdoswald, Castlesteads and Carvoran - soon to be reinforced by a further 500 men from Carrawburgh - can hardly have been expected to see much action in the countryside to the north of their forts, but they were in a position to come to the assistance of either flank cavalry brigade, or to turn south and crush a

Brigantian rising.

The western sector was organised in a similar manner to the eastern sector. Infantry at Drumburgh could deal with routine shore patrols, whilst the cavalry brigade could sweep deep into the north, assisted in this case by troops from the three outpost forts. However restless and disturbed this area was, such troop concentrations should have rendered native resistance impotent.

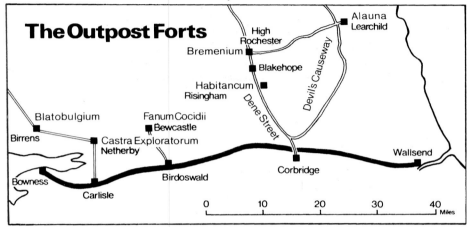

The support forts to the north of the Wall.

To the south of the Wall in the west, and behind the Cumbrian coastal extension of the Wall, there lay another powerful force. The key fort seems to have been Old Carlisle, with its cavalry regiment. The commanding officer at Old Carlisle was senior to the commanders of infantry battalions, and those at Beckfoot, Maryport, Moresby and Papcastle would thus come within his command. He may also have had the responsibility for the tactical role of the garrison at Ravenglass and the presumed force at St. Bees Head. In an emergency, he could thus field a force consisting of a cavalry regiment and four or six infantry battalions, without waiting for instructions from Stanwix, where the senior officer of the Wall commanded the ala Petriana, or from Command Headquarters at York.

The dull routine of Wall and Vallum patrolling and customs supervision were left in the hands of the milecastle garrison. One might have expected that the arrival of regular army units on the line of the Wall would have led to the disbandment of such irregulars, but excavation suggests that they survived as an integral part of the frontier system. To judge by the filthy state of some second century floor levels in the turrets, and by the heaps of rubbish piled against their outside walls (especially outside Turret 25b), the commanding officers in the nearby forts paid little attention to the administration and military discipline of the milecastle garrisons. Gaming counters (Turret 25b), and the use of doorways as hearths (Turret 18b), alongside the evidence of

41

Recruit undergoing weapon training.

rotting piles of bones from stews, suggests a very reduced state of discipline compared with that prevailing inside the forts. But the principal concern of the milecastle garrisons was not military: the refugees and other unauthorised civilians were their targets. Individuals no doubt succeeded in crossing the Vallum at night and perhaps scaling the Wall as well. Some may have bribed the guards, or enrolled friends to create a diversion nearby. We are all too familiar with such necessary stratagems these days, but we have yet to find evidence of a tunnel underneath the frontier. Such a feat of engineering would have been beyond the power of any but Roman army craftsmen.

There is no doubt that the new frontier was immensely powerful, but that power was never chiefly in its physical defences. It was the garrison that affected the native tribesmen to north and south of the Wall, a fast, mobile and hard-hitting task-force, lodged in secure forts. Its effectiveness depended upon training, discipline and morale, and while the high standards of the second century were maintained, no native army could hope to penetrate the province from the north.

Guerilla warefare alone could keep the spirit of resistance alive: ambushes and small-scale skirmishes, too slight to force a major Roman army out into the open, but too cunning and slippery to be defeated by anything short of a scorched earth policy.

We have no evidence about the forms of control exercised by the Romans over the northern tribes after the construction of the Wall, but analogies from better documented frontiers give us the general Roman policy. Tacitus reported the treatment of the Frisii beyond the Rhine frontier, who had to supply ox-hides to the local garrison as tribute, and the unfair definition of what constituted a proper size for the hides led to rebellion. Sometimes the land adjoining the frontier was cleared of its population, and Tacitus records the complaints of the Ampivarii, desperately short of land, whilst that reserved for the army horses and pack animals was not being used at all. Other tribesmen could only cross the frontier after leaving their arms behind and paying a fee - and then they were accompanied by a guard. Sometimes special privileges were granted to a friendly tribe. Beyond the upper Danube frontier the people of the Hermunduri, of proven fidelity to Rome, were allowed to trade across the Danube deep into the province of Raetia. They could enter and leave without guard. Perhaps on the northern frontier, such privileges were granted to the Votadini, whilst savage natives, such as the Caledonians from the mountains, would be forbidden entry.

In effect, a form of stalemate had been acknowledged. Rome could not conquer the whole island, and had fixed a permanent frontier across the most suitable neck of land. While an army could be maintained on that frontier, the remainder of the province was secure. There was always the hope that contact with Roman forces would ultimately persuade more of the northern peoples to enter into alliance and thus secure the benefits of subsidies and privileges. In due course, the size of the army might be reduced.

The emperor in his prime, on a __sestertius__ from the bath house latrine, at Vindolanda.

A small aside on Hadrian's appreciation of the work of his British army must be recorded. When the Emperor was lying seriously ill at his magnificent villa in Italy, Platorius Nepos, his former close friend, who had supervised the building operation when Governor of Britain, asked for permission to visit him. It was refused!! Within weeks Hadrian was dead, and within three years his Wall in Britain had been abandoned. His successor, Antoninus Pius, had ordered the army back into modern Scotland, to construct a new frontier between Forth and Clyde. It was to be only a brief sortie, however, and for most of the long occupation of Britain, Hadrian's Wall was to serve as Rome's northern frontier.

A stone, set in the Wall to record a section constructed by men from Julius Rufus' century.

Further Reading and References

A small library could be filled with works devoted to Hadrian's Wall, which has exercised a special fascination over scholars for the past 400 years. Annual summaries of recent work may be found in volumes of BRITANNIA, published by the Roman Society: general works, which include helpful bibliographies, include Eric Birley, Research on Hadrian's Wall (Kendal, 1961), S.S. Frere, Britannia (London 1967 and later editions) and D. Breeze & B. Dobson, Hadrian's Wall (Harmondsworth 1978). For details of Roman Forts in particular see Anne Johnson, Roman Forts (London 1983). The activities of the garrison are discussed in the companion booklet, Garrison Life on the Northern Frontier.

Acknowledgements

The author acknowledges the assistance of Allison Rutherford, Andrew Birley and the Ermine Street Guard with photographs; Pat Birley with the line drawings, and the late Ronald Embleton with reconstruction drawings.